CLASSROOM TO CAREER

MY JOB IN
SCIENCE

WRITTEN BY
JOANNA BRUNDLE

CONTENTS

WORDS THAT LOOK LIKE THIS CAN BE FOUND IN THE GLOSSARY ON PAGE 31.

BookLife
PUBLISHING

©2020
BookLife Publishing Ltd.
King's Lynn
Norfolk PE30 4LS

All rights reserved.
Printed in Malaysia.

A catalogue record for this book is available from the British Library.

ISBN: 978-1-78637-676-3

Written by:
Joanna Brundle

Edited by:
John Wood

Designed by:
Drue Rintoul

CLASSROOM TO CAREER

At school, your busy day is packed full of different lessons. Some of the most important are STEM subjects. Do you know what they are? STEM stands for science, technology, engineering and maths. So why are STEM subjects so important?

USING STEM

The world moves very fast and it changes all the time. However, STEM can help us understand it. STEM subjects can inspire you to learn more about how the world works, and they might lead to you working in STEM. Lots of new STEM jobs are being created all the time and in all different areas. Who knows what you could be doing in the future? As well as helping you to find interesting work, studying STEM subjects will also help you to solve problems, make decisions and work as part of a team.

A job is something that you do to earn money. Many people stay in jobs for a short amount of time, and they don't always need training. A career is a life-long work journey in an area that really interests you. People often need the right training for the right career.

Dentistry is a life-long career that requires around five years of training.

STEM subjects can help you get into an exciting career, whether you want to be an astronaut, doctor or someone who makes video games. But remember that STEM subjects are important whatever you do. For example, many careers need you to have computer skills. In this book, we are going to look at science and some of the careers it might lead you to. We will be thinking about how you might spend your day and what qualifications and skills you might need.

Science experiments at school could lead to a career as a research scientist.

STEM CAREERS ARE FOR EVERYONE.

MARINE BIOLOGIST

Are you passionate about the natural world? Do you want to make a difference by looking after the environment for people in the future? Are you a keen swimmer or diver? If so, working as a marine biologist could be the career for you. Marine biologists study our seas and oceans and the things that live there, including plants, fish and other animals.

There are many roles within marine biology. Some people study tiny living things called algae, which can only be seen with a <u>microscope</u>. Others protect the giants of the sea, such as the blue whale. Marine biologists may work for charities or for <u>research laboratories</u>. Some work for zoos or sea life centres. Others are employed by companies that drill for oil and gas under the seabed. Marine biologists give these companies information about how to carry out work without damaging the environment.

This marine biologist is checking coral. Coral can be damaged by a rise in sea temperatures caused by <u>climate change</u>.

Marine biologists spend time both at sea and in a laboratory. At sea, they collect and store <u>specimens</u> and check on wildlife numbers, making note of where the animals are and where they are going. In the laboratory, marine biologists use microscopes, computers and other special equipment to study specimens. For example, they might look at the effects of <u>pollution</u> on ocean creatures and plants.

These marine biologists are collecting seawater, which is then studied back at the laboratory.

To become a marine biologist, you will need a <u>degree</u> in marine biology, oceanography (the study of seas and oceans) or environmental science. As well as having a love of the natural world, you will also need to be a strong swimmer and be good at working in a team. You will need to work in a clear and careful way. You may need patience if the weather at sea is against you. It also helps if you like boats!

MARINE BIOLOGY GIVES PEOPLE THE CHANCE TO TRAVEL AROUND THE WORLD.

DOCTOR

If you like the idea of helping people who are sick, then perhaps you should think of becoming a doctor. Doctors are specially trained people whose job it is to look at their patients, figure out what is wrong with them and try to help them get better.

There are many different kinds of doctor. A GP (general practitioner) is often the first type of doctor people will call if they are ill. GPs treat everyday medical conditions, such as infections. They also send patients to hospitals for tests or special treatment. Hospital doctors may work on the wards, in accident and emergency departments or as surgeons. Some doctors are specially trained to care for children or the elderly. Other doctors are specially trained in particular areas of the body, such as the heart or brain.

GPs can see patients at a surgery or at home.

Surgeons are doctors who are specially trained to carry out operations.

It takes a long time to train as a doctor. You need to do very well in school to be able to train to be a doctor. After about five years at medical school, you work as a junior doctor for a few years before deciding what type of doctor you would like to become. You then begin several more years of training in the area you have chosen. Being a doctor can be a difficult career, but also a very important one. You could improve lots of people's lives, and even save lives too.

Some doctors work on air ambulances, helping people who have been in an accident.

As a doctor you might also be able to work abroad because doctors are needed all over the world. Some choose to work for charities, caring for people in parts of the world that are hard to get to. Others work in disaster zones – for example, they might help people who have been caught in an earthquake.

This volunteer doctor is working in Africa.

DOCTORS NEED TO BE KIND AND CARING, AS WELL AS BEING GOOD LISTENERS. THEY MUST ALSO BE CALM AND ABLE TO DEAL WITH DIFFICULT SITUATIONS.

FORENSIC SCIENTIST

A forensic scientist helps to investigate crimes. They search for, collect and study physical <u>evidence</u> from places where crimes have been carried out. Physical evidence includes fingerprints, blood, hair, pieces of clothing, paint, pieces of glass, tyre marks and anything that may have been used to start fires. A forensic scientist will use all these things to work out exactly what happened and who carried out the crime.

Hair being collected to study

At a crime scene, a forensic scientist will take photographs, make sketches and keep written notes of where evidence was found. Each piece of evidence is stored and labelled before being taken to the laboratory. When a forensic scientist is at a crime scene, they wear protective clothing to stop any <u>contamination</u> of the evidence and to protect themselves from anything dangerous.

tective clothing includes an n-one suit, hairnet, mask, es and shoe covers.

SOME FORENSIC SCIENTISTS ARE SPECIALLY TRAINED TO FIND POISONS AND DRUGS.

Evidence that has been collected must be examined in the laboratory. It is often slow, detailed work. Forensic scientists need to work carefully and record all their findings. Physical evidence can link someone who is suspected of having carried out a crime to the crime scene, so there must be no mistakes.

As well as going to crime scenes and working in a laboratory, some forensic scientists also go to law courts to show their findings. They are classed as 'expert' witnesses. This means that they can give an opinion about what they have found, as well as the facts.

Forensic scientists use fingerprint databases to link fingerprints found at crime scenes to suspected criminals.

If being a forensic scientist sounds like the career for you, you will need a degree in biological sciences, chemistry or forensic science. Great attention to detail and being able to keep records is also needed.

RESEARCH SCIENTIST

Do you like finding out new things? Do you enjoy inventing and carrying out experiments of your own, at home or at school? Perhaps the idea of making an important scientific discovery sounds interesting? What about finding a cure or new treatment for a disease or illness? Being a research scientist sounds like the career for you.

These scientists are carrying out research into new medicines.

Research scientists work in all sorts of areas of science. They can also work for lots of different types of employer. You might work for the government, or for a research laboratory that is owned by a company. You could work for an environmental agency or a company that makes and sells products that are sold in shops. Lots of people need research scientists.

Research scientists spend most of their time in the laboratory, where they plan and carry out experiments, and record their results. They use special equipment, including computer software and powerful microscopes. Once they have looked carefully at their results, research scientists write reports that talk about what they have discovered.

A research specialist might use a special microscope like this.

As a research scientist, you might work away from the laboratory, for example collecting soil or water for testing. There are also chances to travel all over the world. You could go to <u>conferences</u>, where you might give a presentation to share your findings with other scientists.

To be a research scientist, you will need a degree in a science subject. A second degree called a master's degree is also helpful. As a person, you will need to be patient, determined and good at working in a team.

A scientist collecting water

ZOOLOGIST

Are you an animal lover? Are you mad about monkeys, in love with llamas or crazy about camels? If so, why not become a zoologist? Zoologists work with animals in their natural habitats and in places such as zoos and aquariums. They study what the animals do, as well as what they eat, and how they have babies. They also study animal diseases.

The work of zoologists is interesting and always different. Some zoologists work to protect <u>endangered species</u> or look after habitats that are under threat.
Other zoologists choose to become specially trained to work with certain animals, such as reptiles, birds or fish. Some run education programmes for adults and children visiting zoos and animal parks. Studying the effects of climate change on the number of animals and their movements is becoming more and more important.

YOU COULD BECOME A SPECIAL TYPE OF ZOOLOGIST, CALLED A PALAEOZOOLOGIST. THEY STUDY ANIMAL <u>FOSSILS</u>.

If you choose to work with animals in places such as zoos and aquariums, you will be in charge of their food and their enclosures. Zoologists try to make sure that the animals' behaviour can be as close as possible to their natural behaviour in the wild.

Zoologists carry out research in the laboratory and outside in the world, where they collect and store specimens to be studied in the laboratory. This work could take you all over the world, including to places that are difficult to get to, such as Antarctica.

You will need a degree in zoology, biology, environmental biology or marine biology to become a zoologist. There are lots of people who want this career, so it might help to get some work experience. You will also need good computer skills as you will be dealing with lots of data and using computer models to study the effects of human behaviour on animal habitats.

SCIENCE TEACHER

The need for people in STEM careers is increasing all the time. How will we have enough people who are qualified to take on these careers? Step forward science teachers of the future.

Science teachers encourage their students to be curious about the world around them and to think about how and why things happen. Science teaching begins when children start school. However, as a science teacher, you may find yourself teaching students of any age. Science teachers write and follow lesson plans, and they also set and mark homework. They make sure that students are taught all that they need to know to pass examinations.

Science teachers know about most areas of science, but they know a lot about one particular subject. For example, they teach an area of science called biology (the study of living t

Goggles

Experiments are an important part of teaching science. Science teachers set up, perform and explain experiments and encourage students to carry out their own. Laboratories can be dangerous places, so science teachers need to make sure their students understand how to work safely, for example using goggles when necessary.

Although science teachers spend most of their time in school, there are chances to work outside the classroom. For example, you might take students on field trips or to science presentations. It is important for you to keep up-to-date, so you may have to go to training sessions yourself.

To be a science teacher, you must have a science degree and be trained to teach children. You will need plenty of patience and enthusiasm and you must be good at talking to students, parents and other staff.

FOOD SCIENTIST

We all need food to stay alive. But have you ever thought about how our food is produced? Who makes sure that it is safe and good for us to eat? This is the role of the food scientist.

Food scientists use their knowledge of science to study our food. They test its flavour, texture and <u>nutritional value</u>. They look at the changes that take place in stored food and find new ways to keep it fresh and tasty. They also investigate ways of saving food companies time and money when making the food. Another important part of a food scientist's work is to test the safety of both uncooked ingredients and finished products. This is to make sure that the companies have followed the government's rules on food safety.

Food scientists spend most of their time working in laboratories.

Have you ever noticed the labels on food that tell you how many <u>calories</u> a food contains, and how much fat, sugar and salt it is made up of? Labels often show how much is in one portion or in 100 grams of the product. Food products are also stamped with 'use by' or 'best before' dates, which tell people when they can safely eat the food or enjoy it at its best. The labels also say which ingredients could cause an <u>allergic reaction</u>. For example, these ingredients could be eggs, wheat or nuts. It is food scientists who work to find out all of this information.

values	100ml contains	250ml contains	%GDA*
ergy	199kJ 47kcal	500kJ 120kcal	6% 20%
	0.5g	1.3g	
rotein	10.5g	26.3g	29%
Carbohydrate	10.5g	26.3g	
of which sugars	trace	trace	
Fat			
of which saturates	trace		
Fibre		trace	
odium		trace	
lt equivalent		trace	
ideline daily amounts			
ins/Minerals		100ml contai	

You will need to work as part of a team.

If you like the idea of being a food scientist, you will need a degree in food science, chemistry, nutrition or microbiology (the study of <u>microbes</u>).

RENEWABLE ENERGY SCIENTIST

Are you passionate about caring for the environment? Are you worried about climate change, and <u>fossil fuels</u> such as coal, oil and gas? If you want to help make energy that is better for the planet, working as a renewable energy scientist could be right for you.

Wind farm

BURNING FOSSIL FUELS PRODUCES A GAS CALLED CARBON DIOXIDE. THIS GAS TRAPS HEAT FROM THE SUN, LEADING TO CLIMATE CHANGE.

Hydroelectric power plant

Renewable energy is energy that comes from any source that does not run out, for example solar (from the Sun), wind and tidal energy. Geothermal plants gather heat from the ground which is used to make steam and <u>generate</u> electricity. Hydroelectric dams use the movement of water to power <u>turbines</u>. Nuclear power is made by something called fission. This involves splitting <u>atoms</u> of a material called uranium. As a renewable energy scientist, you might work for a company or for the government.

Renewable energy scientists develop ways of making renewable energy as useful as possible. As a wind energy scientist, for example, you might be involved in finding a windy location and working out how to position the wind turbines. You might also get involved in environmental issues, looking at ways to ensure a planned wind farm does not damage plant and animal life in the area.

As the need for energy grows, renewable sources such as solar power will become more and more important.

Renewable energy scientists work in the laboratory, in an office and outside. Working outside could mean working in places that are hard to get to, and in all weathers.

At a nuclear plant, you might work in a central control room like this.

In order to be a renewable energy scientist, you will need a science degree in a subject such as physics. Extra training in subjects such as climate science are also helpful. As well as your interest in science, clean energy and the environment, you will also need excellent computer skills.

SPACE SCIENTIST

Does space fascinate you? Would you love to be a space traveller? Have you ever wondered how the universe began and whether there is life on other planets? If so, a career as a space scientist could be right for you. There are many different roles, from rocket designer to astronaut.

Some space scientists study space, including our own solar system and the billions of stars and galaxies that make up the universe. Some design satellites, spacecraft and the equipment that they carry, then plan their launch into space. Others design test programmes and experiments. They study data that is collected from satellites controlled on Earth. They also study results from experiments that have been carried out by astronauts on board spacecraft. Some work on projects exploring distant planets such as Jupiter, using remote control spacecraft and probes. Space scientists might also study the births, lives and deaths of stars, planets, asteroids and other objects in the universe.

A probe called Juno, controlled by a mission team at a space centre, has explored Jupiter's atmosphere.

Some space scientists work as astronauts aboard the International Space Station (ISS). This is a spacecraft with people on it that <u>orbits</u> the Earth every 90 minutes. Its crew of three to six astronauts stay on board for about six months at a time. As well as carrying out all sorts of experiments inside the space station, the astronauts also go on space walks outside the spacecraft. The astronauts study how being in space for long periods of time affects the human body. They also clean, check and repair equipment.

The ISS

If you would like to be a space scientist, you will need a degree in a science subject such as physics. You will also need a further degree in a subject such as astrophysics. Maths, computer and problem-solving skills are also very important.

Space scientists sometimes make discoveries that improve our daily lives. Memory foam used in mattresses, for example, was first used to provide protective, comfortable seats for astronauts.

Astronaut on a spacewalk

METEOROLOGIST

Meteorologists are scientists who study the Earth's climate and weather. They use all sorts of equipment and many scientific skills to record, understand and forecast the weather. Meteorologists also study the causes of particular types of weather, such as hurricanes or tornadoes.

Meteorologists record and study information from worldwide weather stations, weather satellites and weather balloons. They use this data, along with computer models, to forecast both short- and long-term weather patterns. Meteorologists also study the weather over long periods of time, looking at past weather trends to predict what the weather will be in the future.

Weather balloons carry special equipment that measures temperature, wind speed and direction, and the amount of water in the air.

IF YOU THINK THAT A CAREER IN METEOROLOGY IS FOR YOU, YOU WILL NEED A DEGREE IN SCIENCE, COMPUTER SCIENCE, MATHS OR METEOROLOGY.

This satellite is tracking a hurricane.

As a meteorologist, you might work for an environmental agency and research ways to cut down air pollution. You could be employed by a company that needs accurate weather information, such as an aircraft or energy company. You could also work in agriculture, helping crops grow by giving information on weather patterns and trends. A forensic meteorologist might work for companies that help people who have had accidents. This might involve looking at accidents that could have been affected by the weather.

As the effects of climate change continue to get worse, weather forecasting will become more and more important. Dry seasons, high temperatures and strong winds, for example, lead to wildfires. These may put people, animals and buildings in danger. Governments are employing more and more meteorologists to give expert advice on how to plan for and deal with climate change.

SPORT AND EXERCISE SCIENTIST

If you enjoy science but are also passionate about sport, a career in sport and exercise science is for you. Sport and exercise scientists help people to improve their health and fitness. They can also help people to achieve the best possible results in their sport. They do this by using their knowledge of areas such as biomechanics (how the body moves) and physiology (how the body works).

There are many different roles. You can work as a fitness consultant, checking people's fitness and putting together the right exercise programmes for them. If you work with sportspeople, you will carry out tests to measure their performance. After studying the results, you will design full training programmes for them. Some sports scientists work in special medical centres, giving advice on how to treat sports injuries and stop them happening in the first place. Others work with hospitals to help patients who need to become fit again, for example after a heart attack.

Measuring performance

Sport and exercise scientists work in many different pla[ces]. These include gyms and leisure centres, sports med[ical] clinics, training institutes for athletes, and professio[nal] clubs, such as football or ice hockey clubs.

Athlete

Some teach and carry out research in universities. Some work with sports companies, giving expert advice on how to design and make sporting equipme[nt]. Others set up their own clinics or work as personal trainers for people at home. You might be able to do work experience at a summer camp or a football academy abroad.

If you would like to work as a sport and exercis[e] scientist, you will need:

- a degree in sport and exercise science
- further training if you want to work in a particular area, such as nutrition (what food[s] to eat for the best health and fitness)
- the ability to inspire people to work harder and exercise

Working as a volunteer for your local sports club can be rewarding. It can give you valuable work experience.

PHARMACIST

If you enjoy science and like the idea of giving people medicine to help them feel better, then pharmacy could be a good career choice. But there is much more to being a pharmacist than simply taking medicine from a shelf.

Pharmacists prepare, check and package medicine that has been ordered by a doctor. It is the responsibility of a pharmacist to make sure the medicine is high quality and right for the patient. Pharmacists also check patients' symptoms and offer advice and over-the-counter medicine for illnesses such as coughs and colds. Over-the-counter medicines do not need a prescription (a prescription is a note from a doctor that says which medicine is needed). They also help people in other ways by giving them advice on how to live healthier lives. Pharmacists sometimes give advice about medicines to doctors.

Pharmacists work in many different places, including hospitals and community pharmacies. They might work for pharmaceutical companies that research, make and sell medicine. Some work in prisons or in the armed forces. Some work at universities, either in teaching or research. Others train as veterinary pharmacists, providing care for animals.

This pharmacist is explaining the correct use of an asthma inhaler.

It takes around four years to complete a pharmacy degree. As a pharmacist, you will be dealing with lots of different people, including patients and doctors, so you will need to be good at talking to all sorts of people. An important part of the job is explaining to patients why they have to take a certain type of medicine. You will also explain how to take it safely and what the side effects might be.

You will need to be accurate and have an eye for detail, as the decisions you make can have a big impact on patients' lives. Things can get hectic, so you will need to be able to stay calm at all times.

Pharmacists have to keep detailed, accurate records.

SCIENTISTS WHO HAVE CHANGED THE WORLD

STEPHEN HAWKING

Stephen Hawking was a physicist and cosmologist (a scientist who studies the universe). He developed ideas about how the universe began and studied gravity and black holes. His popular science books helped ordinary people to understand complicated ideas. Despite losing the ability to move and speak, he worked throughout his life, talking by using an electronic speech machine.

JACQUES COUSTEAU

Jacques Cousteau was an undersea explorer and marine conservationist (someone who looks after the environment). He co-invented the aqualung, a piece of diving equipment that helped divers to stay underwater for long periods of time. His television documentaries opened up the undersea world to millions of viewers.

JANE GOODALL

Jane Goodall is a scientist who studied chimpanzees for nearly 60 years. She is a world expert, and her discoveries completely changed what we know about chimpanzees. She now works to protect the environment and make more people aware of the threats that chimpanzees face.

TU YOUYOU

Tu Youyou is a scientist who discovered medicine that was very good at fighting malaria. Malaria is a deadly disease that affects people all over the world. Tu Youyou's work has saved millions of lives. She won the 2015 Nobel Prize for Physiology or Medicine.

GLOSSARY

allergic reaction	the body's response to a substance that does not affect most people but causes some to feel unwell
asteroids	small, rocky objects that orbit the sun
atoms	the smallest possible parts of a chemical element
black holes	places in space where the pull of gravity is so strong that nothing, not even light, can escape
calories	units of measurement of the energy in food
climate change	a change in the typical weather or temperature of a large area
computer models	programs created on computers to test real-life situations
conferences	meetings of people with a shared interest that normally take place over several days
contamination	the act of making something unclean or unusable
databases	sets of data held in computers
degree	a qualification in a specialist subject, often given by a university or college to people usually over the age of 18
endangered species	groups of plants or animals that are at risk of extinction (being completely wiped out)
environmental agency	an organisation that protects, manages and conserves the natural world
evidence	proof
fossil fuels	fuels, such as coal, oil and gas, which formed millions of years ago from the remains of animals and plants
fossils	the remains of prehistoric plants or animals that have been preserved in rock
generate	to create, produce or make
gravity	the force that pulls everything downwards towards the centre of large objects in space
microbes	tiny organisms, such as bacteria, too small to be seen with the naked eye
microscope	a piece of scientific equipment used to make objects look many times bigger
nutritional value	the content of food, particularly protein, carbohydrate and fat
orbits	repeatedly travels around another object in space in a curved path
pollution	something in the environment that has harmful or poisonous effects
probes	small spacecraft with nobody on board, sent into space to collect information and send it to scientists on Earth
research laboratories	rooms or buildings used by scientists to carry out experiments in order to discover new information
satellites	machines sent into space to orbit planets, take photographs and collect and send information
specimens	individual animals, plants or samples used for scientific study
turbines	machines with spinning blades for producing electricity
witnesses	people who see a crime take place and give evidence about it

INDEX

Photo Credits

Images are courtesy of Shutterstock.com. With thanks to Getty Images, Thinkstock Photo and iStockphoto.

2&3 – Glinskaja Olga, Victor Metelskiy, Anatolir, Arcady, DRogatnev, VOLYK IEVGENII, Marnikus, Jane Kelly, Idol Design, derter, Anna Frajtova, Nadya_Art, StockVector, tandaV, DRogatnev. 4&5 – sutlafk, michaeljung, Rido, Gorodenkoff, kotoffei. 6&7 – Richard Whitcombe, Bill45, zaferkizilkaya, Merla, Kzenon, Nadya_Art, Babka, Zubada. 8&9 – Monkey Business Images, Dragon Images, Liptak Robert, sqofield, H.Elvin. 10&11 – Sandra Matic, Couperfield, Vladimir Borovic, vchal, Anatolir. 12&13 – stockfour, Akimov Igor, Bildagentur Zoonar GmbH, kosmos111, karnoff. 14&15 – James Kirkikis, Aaronejbull87, Popova Valeriya, Incredible Arctic, Andrew Krasovitckii. 16&17 – Monkey Business Images, AimPix, wavebreakmedia, Halfpoint, artacet, DRogatnev. 18&19 – Hakim Yakoh, Gts, wavebreakmedia, Brian A Jackson, LEDOMSTOCK, Macrovector, angkrit. 20&21 – XXLPhoto, Maxim Burkovskiy, Mark Agnor, Nordroden, Mascha Tace, Amornism, St_art_ai. 22&23 – Vadim Sadovski, Dotted Yeti, 3Dsculptor, Artsiom Petrushenka, Graphiqa Stock. 24&25 – Shimon Bar, aapsky, FrameStockFootages, Christian Roberts-Olsen, Sea Owl, johavel. 26&27 – Gorodenkoff, Jacob Lund, takaimages, Rawpixel.com, Macrovector, Colorlife. 28&29 – wavebreakmedia, AS photo studio, all_about_people, i viewfinder, DRogatnev, AVA Bitter. 30 – The World in HDR, Hans Peters / Anefo [CC0], Tinseltown, Bengt Nyman [CC BY-SA (https://creativecommons.org/licenses/by-sa/4.0)].